Who Was Betsy Ross?

Colleen Adams

Rosen
REAL
READERS

The Rosen Publishing Group, Inc.
New York

Published in 2001 by The Rosen Publishing Group, Inc.
29 East 21st Street, New York, NY 10010

Book Design: Ronald A. Churley

Photo Credits: Cover, pp. 1, 6, 10 © Corbis-Bettmann; p. 4 © Walter Bibikow/FPG International; p. 8 © Catherine Karnow/Corbis; p. 12 © NPNX/Index Stock; p. 14 © Owen Franken/Corbis.

ISBN: 0-8239-8146-0
6-pack ISBN: 0-8239-8548-2

Manufactured in the United States of America

Contents

Family Life

Elizabeth Griscom, also known as Betsy, was born in 1752 in Philadelphia, a city in the British **colony** of Pennsylvania. Betsy grew up in a big family with sixteen brothers and sisters. She helped her mother with cooking, sewing, and taking care of her younger brothers and sisters.

These women are doing chores just like Betsy Ross did when she was growing up.

School Days

Betsy's parents brought her up in the **Quaker** community. They believed in living a simple, peaceful life. Betsy went to school with other Quaker children. She learned reading, writing, math, history, and sewing as part of her school **lessons**.

As a young girl, Betsy learned to sew beautiful quilts and clothing, much like the women in this drawing are doing.

Betsy's Shop

As a young woman, Betsy worked in a shop sewing coverings for chairs, couches, and other **furniture**. She became friends with John Ross, another worker at the shop. Betsy and John married and started their own shop in 1775.

Betsy spent long hours sewing in her shop. She may have looked like the woman pictured here.

The Revolutionary War

Like many **colonists** during this time, Betsy and John did not want to be ruled by England anymore. They wanted the **freedom** to rule their own country. This fight for freedom was called the **Revolutionary War**.

Many colonists were willing to fight for independence from England.

12

George Washington's Visit

General George Washington was an important leader in the Revolutionary War. Many people believe that he visited Betsy in May 1776. He asked her to sew a special flag for the thirteen colonies that were fighting the Revolutionary War. General Washington wanted the flag to have one stripe and one star for each of the thirteen colonies.

Betsy Ross finished the first flag for the United States of America in June 1776.

The American Flag

In July 1776, the thirteen colonies joined together to become the United States of America. On June 14, 1777, Betsy's flag became the official flag of the United States of America. Betsy lived to be 84 years old. She told the story of the first flag to her children and grandchildren, which is why we know of it today.

Glossary

colonist   A person who lives in one country, but is under the rule of another country.

colony   Land that has been settled by a group of people who are ruled by another country.

freedom   The power to do, say, or think what you want.

furniture   Things needed in a room or a house such as beds, chairs, and couches.

lesson   A time during which you study and learn how to do something.

Quaker   A person who follows the beliefs of the Quaker faith.

Revolutionary War   A war that British colonists in North America fought to win freedom from England.

Index